AUCKLAND

Dorothy Perpall
1704 N. Osceola Ave
Clearwater, Florida

Queen Street in the Rain

AUCKLAND

John Castle

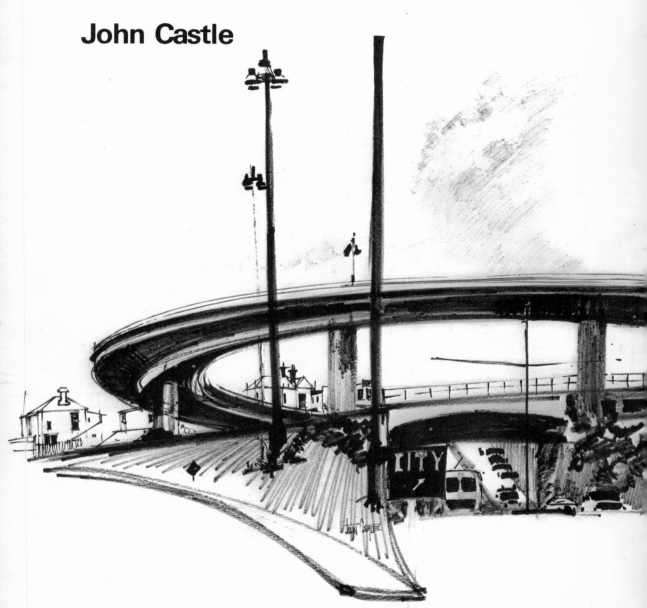

A. H. & A. W. REED: WELLINGTON/AUCKLAND/SYDNEY/MELBOURNE

First published 1970
A. H. & A. W. REED LTD., 182 Wakefield Street,
Wellington; 29 Dacre Street, Auckland; 51 Whiting
Street, Artarmon, Sydney; 357 Little Collins Street,
Melbourne

ISBN: 0 589 00435 2

Set in 10/12 point Times "Monotype" by New Zealand
Typesetters Limited, Wellington. Printed and bound
by Kyodo Printing Company Limited, Tokyo.

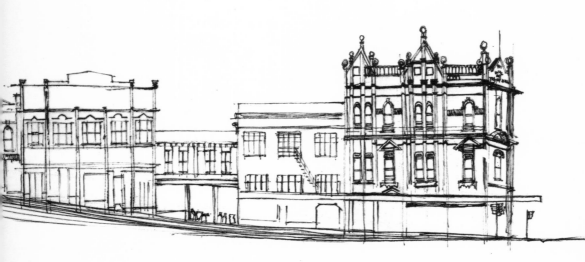

FOREWORD

Auckland is a metropolis with an immense future as a commercial, cultural and tourist centre, set strategically in the South West Pacific, but first it is a city of incomparable beauty.

Countless painters and photographers have recorded its infinite variety of gems for over a century, and in so doing have given us a pictorial history of Auckland's emergence from the earliest colonial times.

John Castle's Auckland is a brilliant summary of much that has gone before, and a sensitive commentary on Auckland as we know it now.

His water colours and sketches should hold a place of pride in the homes of all who love Auckland. This book makes the enjoyment of these illustrations possible for thousands more.

Sir **DOVE-MEYER ROBINSON** (MAYOR)

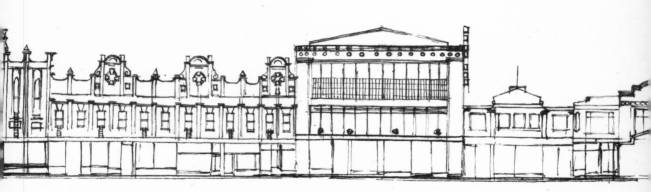

Under the Bridge, Northcote

AUCKLAND, the largest city in New Zealand, occupies a magnificent site between two harbours—the "sparkling Waitemata" and the shallower Manukau. The region on which the city now stands was known to the old Maori as *Tamaki-makau-rau*, the "isthmus coveted by hundreds", an indication of the special esteem in which the area was held. Today that name has gone, yet the area continues to attract new settlers from every other part of New Zealand and many from overseas. Auckland, in the northern third of the North Island, un-questionably is the supreme centre of New Zealand's commerce, industry, population and entertainment. But to sing the city's praises to Aucklanders is unnecessary, for the Aucklander is intensely conscious of his city's beauty and importance.

The city has grown up around a chain of extinct volcanoes which now form a network of beautiful parks and reserves. These green spaces and the many islands visible in the Hauraki Gulf give the city a special character. The most recent of the islands, Rangitoto, "arrived" only eight hundred years ago, and its twin-peaked cone is one of the city's best-known and much-loved landmarks.

The presence of the two harbours is felt from many parts of Auckland. The Waitemata's fleet ranges from canoes to hydrofoils, ocean liners, and men o' war from the Naval Base, and the light craft put out in force particularly at weekends, and on holidays, leaving their moorings and cruising down the harbour. Westhaven, largest mooring area for

Westhaven

7

John Castle

Freighter at Queens Wharf with Tug

the thousands of Auckland pleasure boats, shelters in the lee of the Harbour Bridge. Here is a scene of constant activity during most months of the year as tourists and strollers mingle with the yachties fitting out or launching their boats. Auckland's climate stimulates almost all sports, but water sports in particular—fishing, surfing, sailing, water-skiing, or just lazing in the shade of some great pohutukawa tree on any one of the sun-warmed beaches where the colours of gay umbrellas and bikinis blend with the brightness of sails on the water.

Auckland's climate is semi-tropical and mercurial. On a hot sun drenched summer day, black clouds can suddenly loom up and, without warning, the heavens open. Pedestrians dashing across a Queen Street intersection magically produce umbrellas in a myriad of colours. In a matter of a very few minutes, the rain stops, the sun shines out again, and steam rises from the roadway. Life is back to normal.

Ferry Building

Symonds Street

From the lower end of Queen Street, looking towards the wharves, you may see a towering overseas liner apparently about to sail right up the street. The ship's hull rides high above the traffic passing along Quay Street on the waterfront, and the bustling commerce of the harbourside is integral with the city traffic. Auckland Harbour is by far the busiest in the country, handling every kind of shipping, big and small, and as often as not a number of overseas freighters can be seen anchored out in the harbour awaiting their turn for berthage at the wharves.

The magnificent old lamps of the waterfront still line Quay Street. Like the Ferry Building, they are sturdy reminders of an earlier era of leisure and elegance. The Ferry Building, completed in 1912, was the terminal for the many harbour ferries, but these seaborne services passed into history with the completion of the Harbour Bridge, which gives quick road access to the North Shore suburbs and the Northland coasts and countryside. A regular ferry to Devonport is still maintained, and the old ferries are often used for harbour cruises. New services to the outlying island resorts of the Hauraki Gulf including a hydrofoil and a fleet of amphibian aircraft have largely taken the old ferries' place as sea-carriers of passengers and freight.

Town Hall, Administration Building

The old building in the centre was about to be demolished when
I painted this, and I was glad to be able to record it before it
was too late.

Symonds Street though so close to Queen Street, is very reminiscent of early Auckland. Here many of the first prominent citizens built their homes. Trees from "Home" were planted along the street, the birds sang, the polished horsedrawn carriages passed proudly to and fro. Now each corner is stamped with the red, amber and green of traffic lights, car and truck engines race noisily, and the bulldozers growl and bellow as they cut down the old residences in preparation for yet another streamlined faculty block for the University.

The Town Hall built in 1911 with its classic pillars and charming clock tower dominated the Queen Street skyline until recently. Now its period charm is actually enhanced by the towering simplicity of the new City Council administration building. From the lookout on the top floor of this building you may linger and memorise the finest views across the city and harbour.

It is a fallacy that Auckland was named after the Great Auk bird, for it was in fact named after George Eden, the first Lord Auckland, who was responsible for appointing Captain Hobson, founder of the city to his first naval command. A fine statue of Lord Auckland is to replace the old Market Hotel shown in the centre of the painting on page 11.

Freemans Bay—Changing scene

Ponsonby, with the Post Office tower in the centre.

Durham Street West

Opposite page: Emily Place

Lunchtime in Albert Park

In its Art Gallery, and also displayed in its many parks and green areas around the city, Auckland boasts much good sculpture, both traditional and modern. It is fitting that many are outdoor works, to be enjoyed by all who pass by in this, New Zealand's most "outdoor" city.

Originally the city shoreline was a series of bays. In the west, Freemans Bay; then Commercial Bay (now the downtown city area); Official Bay, principal home of the Government officials or "Red Tape" as the settlers ruefully called them; and Mechanics Bay, where the timber-sawyers worked, now the site of many large warehouses and the steel maze of the railway yards. Now, because of reclamation, Quay Street follows the waterfront and the bays themselves are merely a fading memory. Fort Street followed the foreshore line in the early days, and customers wishing to enter shops here often had to wait for

Mission Bay

Across St Heliers to Rangitoto

the waves to recede before making a dash for the doorways. Work began on reclaiming Commercial Bay in 1859 and it was filled in as far as Customs Street, which for some time became the waterfront. In 1872 Point Britomart was cut back as far as Emily Place, and the spoil was used to form a level area for Auckland's first railway station. By 1873 the Auckland-Penrose-Onehunga line was in use.

Auckland is still a city in transition. This can be seen in every sector of the city, where modern commercial and industrial buildings are everywhere rising in construction. Along the waterfront on Quay Street the mammoth Downtown Development includes a large tourist hotel, the new Customhouse, a parking building, and a building for an international airline, and will undoubtedly change the silhouette from the harbour.

Cranes on the skyline are a commonplace, slowly swinging their long arms, looking like giant fretwork birds. The strong simplicity of design achieved in the new buildings are in sharp contrast with those constructed before the Second World War. In turn these are markedly more functional than the ornately decorative buildings common around the turn of the century and earlier.

Early this century the new Grafton Bridge was the longest single-span concrete bridge in the world; today it still carries a remarkable volume of heavy traffic. Beside the bridge, shaded by quiet English trees, is a graveyard, the burial place of many prominent early settlers and of Captain William Hobson, the first Governor of New Zealand. Hobson chose Auckland as the site of New Zealand's new capital, and on 18 September 1840 his officers proclaimed its founding at a formal ceremony. The purchase price from the Maoris was £56 in cash, plus a collection of blankets, trousers, shirts, waistcoats, caps, casks of tobacco, pipes, yards of gown pieces, iron pots, hatchets, one bag of sugar, and one bag of flour. Only a year later 143 lots of land were sold to settlers for a total of £21,299 9s 0d.

Ewelme Cottage

Parnell Shops

St Matthews

Auckland Grammar School

Of the many bridges and viaducts in Auckland today the best known and most prominent is undoubtedly, the Harbour Bridge. It was opened in 1959 with four traffic lanes and has since been extended to eight lanes in order to carry the ever-increasing traffic between Auckland and the North Shore beaches and bays. The additions, made by a Japanese firm, are affectionately known to Aucklanders as "the Nippon Clip-on".

The Auckland Bridge Authority operates the Harbour Bridge, with its approaches and the toll plaza, on lines similar to those used in San Francisco. It is a common sight to see one of the red Authority vehicles servicing part of the bridge equipment, or quietly towing away a disabled car—all with a minimum of fuss or delay and a maximum of speed and courteous efficiency.

The Manukau from Blockhouse Bay

The city's modern system of roads has been an example to the rest of New Zealand. Wide motorways spread for many miles both north and south of the city, and overpasses and viaducts allow the motorist to reach the heart of the downtown area with surprising speed and ease. The city and suburban roads are wide, and improvements are constantly being made to keep the ever-increasing volume of traffic flowing freely.

The suburbs of Auckland continue to spread north and south of the central city complex across the extensive areas of land available for building. On the North Shore the suburbs of Takapuna, Milford and the bays beyond despite a booming rate of growth still have something of the atmosphere of the seaside holiday centres they used to be. To the south, a large industrial centre has developed; the boroughs of Otahuhu and Papakura and the cities of Papatoetoe and Manukau (with Manurewa as its centre) have grown outwards towards each other until they almost meet. A tour along Tamaki Drive around the harbour edge takes one through the eastern suburbs and beaches of Mission Bay, Kohimarama and St Heliers, and ultimately to the suburbs of the Tamaki Estuary. In the north-west the suburbs stretch out to Titirangi in the bush-clad Waitakere Ranges and the wine-growing Henderson Valley, then on to the Memorial Park and the popular beaches of the West Coast.

22

Opposite page: Polynesian Sunday—Ponsonby

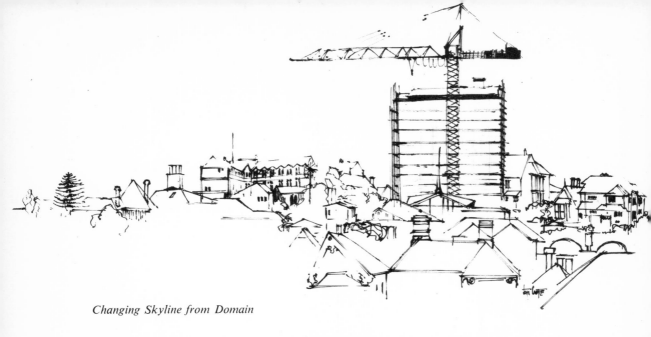

Changing Skyline from Domain

Whether suburbs, boroughs or cities in their own right, most outer suburbs have a sense of space and generous dimension. It is claimed that of all the world's cities Auckland is third largest in actual area and this advantage is clearly seen in that roomy, airy homes, set in their own gay gardens or even in bush settings, are not uncommon. Lush tropical plants such as banana palms and hibiscus grow in many gardens. Trees are everywhere, and shopping, whether in one of the friendly modern market centres that have sprung up through the suburbs, or in the large number of bright specialty shops available, is always a pleasure.

Of the inner, older suburbs, most have retained the charm and character which they established at the turn of the century. Older houses fronting the water or with harbour views are still delightful places in which to live. Many have been restored and modernised and form a happy balance between the old and the new way of urban living.

Old Shops—Newton

In Ponsonby, Freemans Bay and Newton the character changes sharply again, for here is the world's Polynesian centre. Here small houses are grouped tightly together, frequently occupied by many people. However, redevelopment schemes are in progress and the older dwellings are being replaced by modern town houses or apartment blocks.

Over the past twenty-five years 30,000 Polynesians have migrated to New Zealand from their island homes in search of a future with better opportunities in work and education. More than two-thirds of these people have settled in Auckland. Their numbers added to the resident Maori population (which a high natural birthrate and internal migration is steadily increasing), give Auckland a larger Polynesian

Houses—New Suburb

population than that of any other city in the world. Life in a new land is never very easy, and high rentals for low-standard accommodation, language barriers, and initial lack of understanding of New Zealand's regulated social ways are some of the difficulties that Islanders have learned to face and overcome, and they are widely liked and respected for their devotion to their families and their churches.

Greenlane Hospital and One Tree Hill from Cornwall Park

The Maori name for Auckland, *Tamaki-makau-rau* has also been translated as "city of a thousand lovers". When one strolls through Albert Park at lunchtimes and weekends it can indeed be seen why, for this green, city-centre park fills with young and not-so-young couples lunching on the fruits of love, regardless and usually blissfully unaware of being observed from the University and other nearby vantage points.

Many of Auckland's parks are on and around extinct volcanoes and give excellent views over the city. On Mount Eden, high above the bustle of the city, the silent crater with its steep walls and piles of weathered scoria is a reminder of the molten inferno that the whole isthmus must have once been and, of the land's emptiness as the fires died away and vegetation became established– its peace and quiet later to be shattered by the tumult of Maori settlement and bitter warfare, subsiding only when the Pakeha arrived.

In Cornwall Park, whilst watching sheep grazing alongside white-flannelled cricketers, one may look up at the summit of One Tree Hill to the obelisk marking the grave of Sir John Logan Campbell, "Father of Auckland", and perhaps speculate on the life-span of the lone twisted pine still standing there. One of the original merchants of Auckland Sir John gave this park to the city in 1901 to commemorate the visit of the Duke and Duchess of Cornwall and York. His original city store, first erected in what is now Shortland Street, now stands in Cornwall Park.

Opposite page: Newmarket at Night

Old House—Herne Bay

Another pioneer cottage in Cornwall Park is the cricket clubhouse, a recent donation by a leading citizen in memory of his son, and transported from another part of the city. The same family were also responsible for helping in the preservation of Partington's Mill, an Auckland landmark from 1851 until 1950, until it had to be removed.

Aucklanders have a deep sense of pride in their heritage, and many groups and individuals are active preserving that which is old and historical. One such group have raised the money to restore and open to the public, a cottage built in 1863, an excellent example of an old wooden house of the period and largely unchanged since its construction.

From Devonport—Early Morning

29

Grafton Bridge

The War Memorial Museum in the Domain houses fine collections of Pacific Island and Maori as well as other notable exhibits, and a fine library. Alongside it are the Winter Garden, playing fields and quiet walks, whilst adjoining the Domain is the Auckland Public Hospital, one of the many hospitals of which Auckland is justly proud and which have earned for the city world renown in the field of medicine, and, more especially, surgery.

Mission Bay, one of the city beaches, takes its name from the Melanesian mission home established there in 1859. The original stone mission house still stands at the western end of the beach amongst huge Norfolk pines planted by the pioneers. Another feature of this bay is the memorial fountain. A bequest to the city, it takes thirty-nine hours of continuous playing to complete its cycle of jets and colour combinations.

Auckland's night scene is dramatic. The changing blues of the sea by day become black velvet at night, reflecting the thousands of twinkling white house street lights on either shore, spanned by the blaze of yellow lights across the bridge. The noises of industry are hushed and those of fun-loving Aucklanders at play take their place. Commercial signs blaze and flash their messages with mechanical insistance whilst in the streets below citizens and visitors mingle in a human cocktail searching for *la Dolce Vita* in the city's nightspots.

Toll Plaza at Dusk

If the city's night life reflects the affluence of the Aucklander, this quality becomes even more obvious on Regatta Day (Auckland Anniversary Day). Thousands of yachts, from mini-cockleshells to majestic keelers take to the water, many of them competing in what has become the world's biggest single-day regatta. The shores of the Waitemata are crowded with people, families and friends of those racing and others just wishing to watch—after all, what better way to spend an Anniversary Day than in the Auckland suns?

This is a majestic city. The Aucklander may take pride in his citizenship. If the official capital now lies somewhere there down south, he feels no envy, no regret: Auckland is, as she always has been, New Zealand's greatest and fastest growing city—capital in importance, capital in wealth and beauty.

Awaiting the Barnesdance